Richard Illing

JAPANESE EROTIC ART
AND THE LIFE OF THE COURTESAN

With 41 color plates

GALLERY BOOKS
An Imprint of W. H. Smith Publishers Inc.
112 Madison Avenue
New York City 10016

Published by Gallery Books
An imprint of W.H. Smith Publishers Inc.
112 Madison Avenue
New York, New York 10016

This book was designed and produced by
Blacker Calmann Cooper Ltd, London

Reprinted 1983

Library of Congress Cataloging in Publication Data
Main entry under title:
Japanese erotic art.
        1. Erotic art — Japan. 2. Prints, Japanese. 3. Scrolls, Japanese.
I. Illing, Richard.
N7350.J34   760   78-19949

ISBN 0-8317-2889-2

Printed in Spain by Graficromo S.A.

Introduction

THROUGHOUT THE LATTER HALF of the seventeenth, the eighteenth and the nineteenth centuries, the Japanese courtesan, her beauty, her skills, her fashions and every detail of her life were objects of consuming interest and fascination in the gay life of Edo, now the modern city of Tokyo. In the entertainment world of a society whose hedonistic morality was founded on a belief in the transient nature of life, the top-ranking courtesans were the feminine equivalent of today's film stars and pop stars. Famous popular artists vied with one another to make them the subjects of prints that are now acknowledged to be masterpieces of graphic art. Since the Japanese had never considered that sexual enjoyment was something to which shame should be attached, these same artists did not hesitate to show the sex-life of the girls and in doing so produced some of the most beautiful evocations of passionate love that the world has ever seen. Their art is the subject of this book.

The works themselves can broadly be divided into two categories. There were guides to the pleasure quarters and pictures of the inmates, the courtesans and their apprentices, the geishas, the tea-house girls and the entertainers. In these, erotic overtones, although present to the discerning eye, are not explicit. Also, forming a distinct sub-group, were the overtly erotic sex pictures, '. . . a predominantly serious, artistic glorification of the erotic, as far removed from phallic-religious significance as it was from snickering prurience. It was a clean and open art-form, enjoyed, without guilt, by a race to whom the full pleasures of sex were considered but one of the natural rights of mankind.' (Richard Lane, *The Erotic Art of the East*, ed. Philip Rawson.) The Japanese called them *shunga* or 'spring pictures'. Relative freedom from political, religious or public prejudice meant that the artists could take pride in producing pictures of sexual life which were expressly intended to give pleasure to the viewer.

To place the situation of the courtesan in perspective it is necessary to know something of the historical background. During the Middle Ages Japan had been subjected to long periods of destructive civil war. Clan fought against clan with a relentless intensity which was typically Japanese. Implacable warriors of great courage and fanatical loyalty killed each other as armies strove mercilessly to annihilate their opponents. The country was ravaged and impoverished. These struggles culminated in the rise to power of the warlord Ieyasu. After an overwhelming victory in 1600 he set up a government in Edo and established a military dictatorship which was maintained by his descendants from the Tokugawa clan until the middle of the nineteenth century, when internal pressures and the arrival of the warships of the Western trading powers undermined their influence and caused their downfall in 1867. For more than two and a half centuries, however, the Tokugawa *shoguns*, with an impregnable fortress as their power-base in Edo and a self-imposed seclusion from the rest of the world, faced little chance of opposition. The titular head of the nation was still the Emperor but he and his court, tucked away in the beautiful old inland city of Kyoto, had no real power and successive Emperors remained only as ceremonial figures.

The *shoguns* used their power to consolidate their position. They strengthened the old rules of society with new laws, actively promoting distinctions between classes. The *samurai*, less than ten per cent of the population, were a military caste of nobles, knights and retainers, inculcated from birth with a sense of superiority and governed by ideals of loyalty and a rigid adherence to duty. They became increasingly anachronistic and underemployed during the years of imposed peace. They were paid fixed stipends based on units of the staple commodity, rice. The peasant farmer, theoretically second in the order of classes, was the producer of such wealth. In practice he was a poor man, who worked from dawn to dusk, knelt with his forehead on the ground when his lord went by, and was heavily taxed. Although scorned as the third and lowest class, the middlemen, who serviced the wealth produced by the farmers and spent by the *samurai*, prospered with the peace and tended to become rich. These were the townsmen, the builders and craftsmen, the bankers and merchants and the servants and shopkeepers. Restricted by sumptuary laws in how they might spend their new-found wealth, the townsmen now had the leisure and opportunity to study and to develop a popular lowbrow taste in literature, poetry and drama. With these new interests to prompt them, they looked increasingly for amusement and entertainment.

What was the position of the women in this society? A married woman played a subservient role in the home of her husband's family. She was governed by the 'three obediences'; as a child to her father, as a wife to her husband, as a widow to her eldest son. Although these rules tended to be followed more strictly in the *samurai* families, marriages were usually arranged and were based on duty and respect rather than love. Sex in marriage was primarily intended to lead to procreation; barrenness in a wife was grounds for divorce. For the men, however, facilities were available outside marriage for sexual encounters of a more 'romantic' and sophisticated kind.

Prostitution, in one form or another, had always been rife in Edo, a 'city of bachelors', but with the coming of peace arose the Yoshiwara, a legitimate, regulated, enclosed brothel quarter, where the degree of refinement surrounding an evening's indulgence was limited only by the depth of one's purse. Designed to please all the senses, with trees and flowers, processions and celebrations, it was a place where, as night fell, the lanterns were lit and the gaiety, the songs, the music and the dancing began. This is where you could meet the 'men of the moment', artists, authors, poets, thinkers and indeed everyone who was engaged in the pursuit of pleasure. The Yoshiwara was, above all, somewhere where all men, of whatever class, could rub shoulders as equals, so long as they could pay their bills. Situated on the north-east boundary of Edo, the Yoshiwara was a walled enclave, entered through a single gate, under the jurisdiction of the town magistrates. Beyond the gate was a broad central thoroughfare planted with cherry trees. 'Handsome two-storeyed wooden buildings, open to the street, were filled with pretty young girls, playing upon the *samisen* (banjo), having their hair dressed, sitting idle, or engaged at their toilet mirrors . . . streets of neat houses extended to a distance of half a mile on each side, from which the same sounds proceeded.' (W. E. Griffis, *The Mikado's Empire*, New York 1876.) Thus wrote a visitor to Edo in 1871, when the Yoshiwara contained over one hundred and fifty brothels, about four hundred tea-houses serving as inns for assignations with higher class courtesans, and more than three thousand registered prostitutes of all grades. The girls, classified according to their beauty, skills and cost, had usually served an apprenticeship to an established courtesan for several years before starting their careers at the age of about fifteen. They were usually either one of the products of the secret maternity hospitals, run for the prostitutes by the brothel proprietors, or the daughters of penurious peasants sold to travelling procurers in childhood. There were also many stories of women who sold themselves into bondage to provide for a sick husband, an impoverished family or ailing aged parents.

An evening's entertainment would often start with a short trip by boat along the Sumida river. Horses could be hired for the final mile along a wide embankment between rice fields. The Yoshiwara at night was brightly lit by a myriad of paper lanterns and was full of a bustling throng of customers, sightseers, pimps, street-vendors and servants. Lower ranking courtesans, gorgeously dressed and made up, sat in rows in the ground floor apartments of the often palatial mansions. The rooms were open to the street but protected from the outside by grilles of wooden bars. To make an assignation with one of the higher ranking girls an intermediary had to be hired at one of the tea-houses. After sake had been served the visitor would be shown a 'menu' of the available girls and, especially if a newcomer, advised of their particular charms. He would be expected to pay without hesitation, to tip well and to expect no change. The tea-house girl would not only arrange the meeting but would act as the customer's personal attendant for the evening, ordering food, drink and entertainment and later guiding him to his bed-chamber. The courtesan's training would include not only expert sexual technique but also conversation, repartee and all the arts of agreeable companionship to keep the client amused during the evening's entertainment in preparation for the night's events. Some visitors, interested only in the conviviality, singing, dancing and games, would leave before the gates were closed at midnight. Most stayed overnight with one of the girls. Rising at first light they returned home early, pausing for a moment at the 'Gazing back willow', for a last glimpse of the scene of their pleasures. The bill would have been a heavy one and, unless they were very rich, they would not be able to come frequently. Indeed, public opinion which viewed with equanimity the pursuit of sexual pleasure, eyed with disquiet the money that was sometimes squandered. Young rakes were apt to ruin both themselves and their families and there are many stories of older men who did the same, for the Yoshiwara was expert at the game of parting men from their money.

The intelligent, witty and accomplished girls of the highest rank, the idols of this artificial world of sensual pleasure, formed only a tiny proportion of the inmates but, by setting the highest standards at the top, their presence exerted an influence on those who strove to emulate them. The favours of this handful of cultured beauties were reserved for the very rich, the nobles, the court officials, the wealthiest bankers and merchants. Here the despised townsman was able to buy the elegance and romantic refinement which his lowly status outside denied him, however rich he might be. The courtesan expected to be courted by her client and a man who failed to do so would be made to feel ridiculous. The higher the status of the courtesan the greater the degree of flirtation and seduction expected. In the case of the top grades, the *oiran* might require several visits, with expensive gifts and exchanges of love letters, before she would succumb. For all these girls, their entire world confined within the walls of the Yoshiwara, the only chance of romance lay in their transient affairs with the men that came and went in their lives; there is abundant evidence that these close and intimate relationships between young men and women often involved the emotions of both. Vows of fidelity were exchanged, love letters and poems composed, mutual gifts of locks of hair were wrapped in ribbon and sewn into their garments and both men and women frequently fell in love with each other.

Despite these pathetic, transient romances, life for the courtesan was mainly an unpleasant form of female slavery. Once within the walls of the Yoshiwara she became entangled by debts that she could never hope to repay, and the walls, the regulations and the guard on the gate combined to make escape an impracticable dream. Her only possible road to freedom lay in the remote chance that a rich admirer would one day purchase her freedom and marry her. It is happy to relate that this did happen occasionally, sufficiently often to keep hope alive, sufficiently rarely for each case to have been faithfully recorded. Otherwise, the sad truth remains that the courtesan was a prostitute, living in a gilded cage where life was little different from that of other prostitutes in brothels throughout history.

For generations the girls of the Yoshiwara provided subject-matter for the commercial artists who designed the popular woodblock printed broadsheets and illustrated books. I have selected works mainly from the forty years following the introduction of full colour printing in 1764, a period which contains the cream of Japanese colour printed *shunga*, the erotica, and *bijin-e*, 'pictures of pretty girls'. It covers the pictures of the slim, fragile-looking little girls of Harunobu and Koriusai and the 'golden age' of figure prints when Utamaro and a galaxy of other talented artists competed with each other to produce ever more beautiful, technically dazzling designs of the most fashionable women of the day. The *bijin-e*, often named portraits of famous courtesans, were in great demand at all times until they were restricted by censorship laws in 1842. Sets of single sheet prints were usually linked by a fanciful title or theme and could be bought as a set or separately. Where the artist needed a broader spread, prints would be designed and sold as diptychs or triptychs. Print dimensions tended to conform to conventional paper sizes and were restricted by the size of woodblock that could be conveniently worked. Emphasis was often placed on the stylish coiffeur and the patterns and cut of the garments, both of which played an important part in feminine attraction. The leading courtesans were arbiters of ladies' fashions and prints showing these girls performed an important subsidiary role by acting as fashion plates. No artist could afford to ignore the newest vogue in hair styling or the latest extravagance in the printed or embroidered materials of the kimono. Beneath the kimono was worn a long under-dress, often with a contrasting lining and much stress was laid on the taste shown by the choice of colours and patterns of these robes and of the *obi*, the broad sash which held the kimono gathered at the waist. The tying of the *obi* was itself of significance since, although anciently always tied in the front, from the mid-eighteenth century this custom was restricted to the courtesans. The use of cosmetics is also often shown. The practice of blackening the teeth, traditionally a sign of married status, is also seen in prints of courtesans, who were sometimes called *ichitya-zuma*, 'one night wives', on the theory that they were married to their clients, albeit only for a night.

The accent on costume only partly explains the relative lack of the nude in Japanese art as a whole and in the *shunga* in particular. In the latter, the figures were usually draped but with the genitals exposed to reveal details of the sexual activity; this served to concentrate the attention on the sensual focus which was at the heart of the design. Nudity was rarely, of itself, erotic to the Japanese. In a culture where communal bathing was usual, nakedness was too common to be exciting. It is apparent that the viewers of the *shunga* would also have had no illusions about the true dimensions of the genital organs, which artistic convention always exaggerated enormously. Even the most inexperienced bride (sometimes the avowedly intended recipient of *shunga* books and albums) would not have been so unworldly as to have been deceived by these pictures.

The erotic prints tended to be mounted, folded, in sets in albums and were meant to be viewed consecutively, much in the way that a hand-scroll would be unrolled section by section to show one scene at a time. Some *shunga* prints were mounted in a roll in this way but this was less usual. These sets commonly consisted of twelve designs, of which the first and sometimes one or two others were not overtly sexual. Variations in type of sexual activity, posture and setting avoided the risk of wearying the eye with unrelieved coitus. The linear, two-dimensional quality of Japanese draughtsmanship allowed them to show a scene as if drawn from several simultaneous vantage points. This was helpful in depicting sexual intercourse as it is difficult, using Western naturalism and perspective, to maintain visual logic without having to restrict the postures shown and the angles of view. The Japanese artist, however, was unrestricted by the rules of perspective and able to use draped clothing to distract the eye from unusual positions of limbs. Even considerably distorted anatomy was frequently accepted without apparent awkwardness.

Many of the erotic works were promoted for their instructional matter, claiming artistic descent from the 'pillow books' and scrolls handed on as family heirlooms to noble brides. Certainly part of the *shunga* booksellers' steady sales came from their widespread use as gifts to newlyweds. All the techniques of preliminary foreplay and arousal are given prominence, with every indication that as much attention was paid to ensuring the enjoyment of the female partner as to that of the male. They do not, therefore, seem to have served only as a vicarious outlet for the immature or the sexually deprived. In addition to the urban booksellers' market, travelling pedlars seem to have had a steady sale to housewives in the country districts and there is little doubt that ordinary families used *shunga* as an aid to arousal and to heighten stimulation in their everyday sexual relations. That they played a significant part in basic sex education is less certain. The Japanese house, with walls literally paper-thin, was no place for secretive behaviour, even had social custom demanded it, and children would scarcely have had to be taught the 'facts of life'.

The overall impression gained from these pictures of life in old Edo is one of a gay, fun-loving society, which took pains to ensure that the joys of sex were savoured to the full. These prints, by famous artists, make that world come alive again, showing us the beauty and elegance of the courtesans, and the gusto and *joie de vivre* with which life was pursued.

1. *Utamaro* (1754–1806)

1804. From 'Annals of the green houses'; colour-printed book illustration. 7 × 10½ in (18 × 26·5cm)

Dusk is falling and, in the first floor apartment of one of the houses of the Yoshiwara, the lanterns have already been lit. Four men are sitting, gazing out at the moon rising over the broad, raised causeway which, running between rice fields, connected the Yoshiwara with the city of Edo. One of their courtesans has already joined the party and a second, her green *obi* tied prominently in the front, is approaching. The two other girls remain temporarily aloof, chatting to each other. In the foreground the boundary wall of the Yoshiwara is topped by a prominent row of sharp pointed stakes.

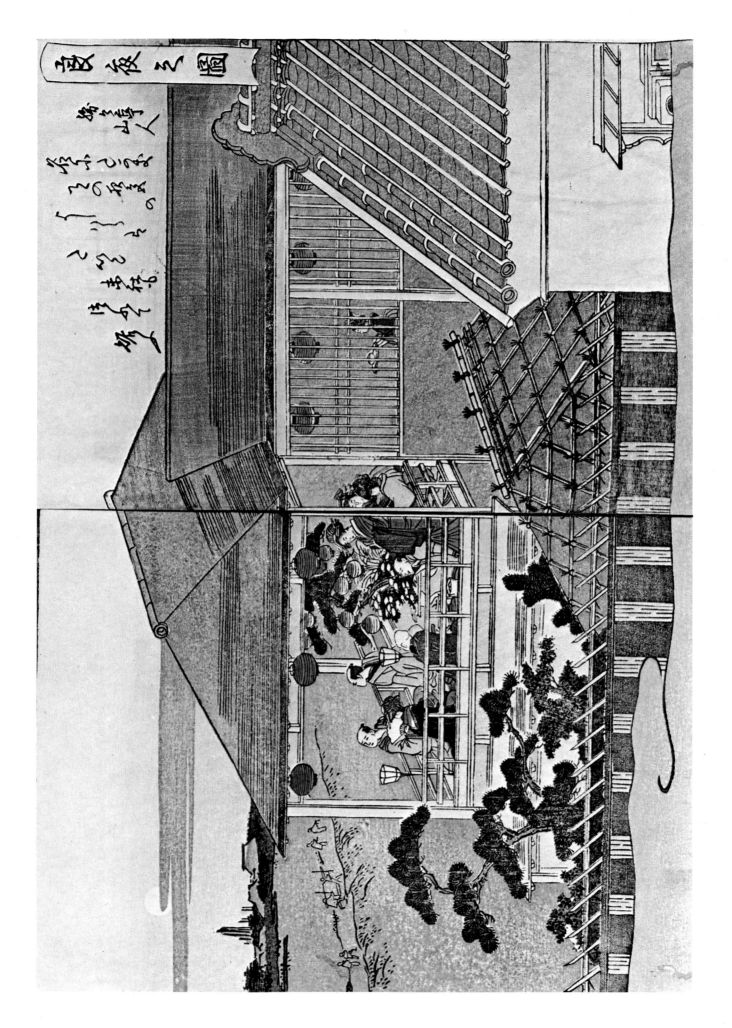

2. *Utamaro* (1754–1806)

c.1800. From 'Celebrated beauties compared with the
Chushingura'; oban colour print. c.15 × 9in (38 × 23cm)

Utamaro designed several prints which are thought to be
self-portraits but here we are left in no doubt. The two
characters of his name appear in roundels on his robe
and an inscription on the post above reads, 'By request
Utamaro draws his charming face'.

The series is a parody on the famous *Kabuki* play
Chushingura and this print, illustrating Act XI, alludes to
the villain Moronao, who is discovered at night by the
victorious heroes and subsequently executed. This more
convivial scene shows him being plied with *sake* by
three elegant courtesans; his approaching fate is left to
our imagination.

3. *Utamaro* (1754–1806)

1804. From 'Annals of the green houses'; colour-printed book illustration. c.7½ × 10½in (19 × 26·5cm)

In the print above, Utamaro has given us a further portrait of himself within the Yoshiwara. Here, however, he has shown himself at work, decorating an entire wall of the Ogiya (House of the Fan) with a huge picture of a Ho-ho bird, a Chinese mythological beast akin to a phoenix, half pheasant, half peacock. Spread on the floor about him are bowls containing the prepared pigments and a triple-tiered box holding pots of unmixed colours and trays full of brushes. A servant boy tends the charcoal brazier and through the sliding door a bunch of curious courtesans look on fascinated.

The print below shows the ceremonial 'graduation' of *shinzo*, or 'newly made' courtesans, which was an important event in the Yoshiwara. After their years of apprenticeship as *kaburo* the girls, when ready, would be dressed in new finery and, during a week of celebrations, would be paraded publicly through the Yoshiwara each evening. Preceded by a servant carrying a lantern, the four young girls, in identical kimonos, are followed by their sponsoring *oiran* flanked by her two *kaburo* and followed by other members of the House and servants. Everywhere the fan motif of the Ogi-ya (House of the Fan) can be seen advertising its presence.

4. Anonymous

Early eighteenth century. Part of a hand-painted scroll;
colours on silk. $8\frac{1}{4} \times 5\frac{3}{4}$ in (21 × 14·5cm)

Although the work of the print artists is, by virtue of the
medium, more widely known for the prints than their
original paintings, most of the artists also executed
private commissions for wealthy patrons. Hand-painted
shunga scrolls are known to have been popular in
aristocratic and court circles from as early as the Heian
period (eighth to twelfth centuries AD). This is but one
design from a *shunga* scroll in *Ukiyo-e* style and probably
dates from the early eighteenth century. It is unsigned.

5. *Harunobu* (1724–1770)

1770. From 'A comparison of beauties of the green houses';
colour-printed book illustration. c.7½ × 10½in (19 × 26·5cm)

The slim-wristed, winsome beauties of Harunobu form one of the high points of early colour printing in Japan. This illustration shows the courtesan Shiratama, one of the higher grade girls of the Tama-ya (House of the Jewel). She is half-kneeling, holding a *samisen*, warmly wrapped in an elegant winter robe patterned with snow-laden bamboo. Her personal crest (*mon*), a formalized *glycinia* bloom, is emblazoned on her sleeve. The picture comes from a superb five-volume work portraying over one hundred and sixty Yoshiwara beauties, each inscribed with a seasonal *haiku* verse by Kasaya Saren.

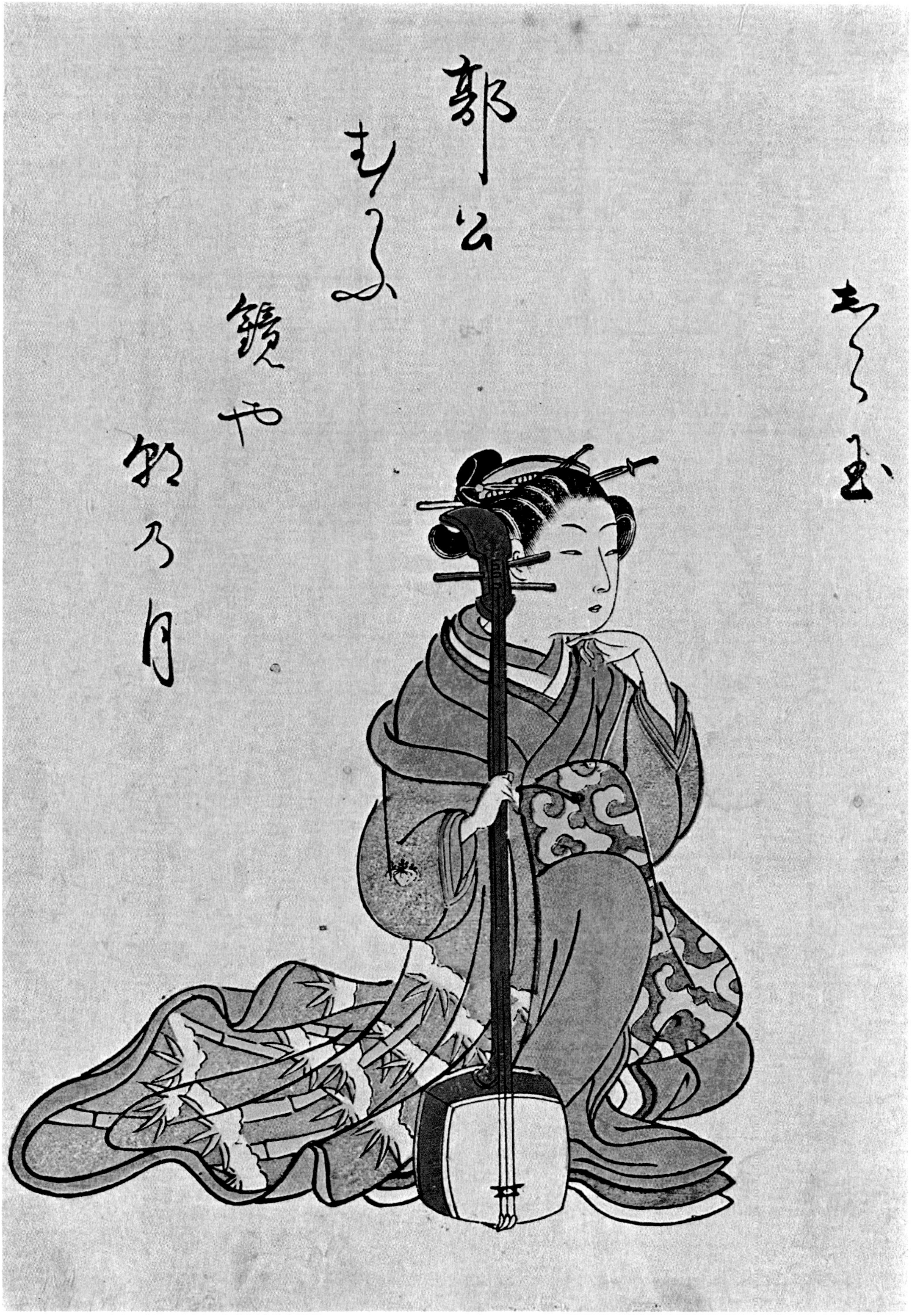

6. *Buncho* (active 1765–1775)

Early 1770s. Chuban colour print. c.$9\frac{3}{4} \times 7\frac{1}{2}$in (25 $\times$19cm)

This relaxed, intimate scene shows two lovers reclining on a triple-tiered mattress. They are listening to the *hototogisu*, a songbird redolent with romantic imagery and almost emblematic of the balmy days of summer. The man is filling his pipe from a tobacco pouch. In front of him is a lacquer *tabako-bon*, containing smoking requisites. Beside the girl is a wad of folded paper tissues which have a definite erotic connotation. They would be used after love-making and their presence here, neatly folded, indicates that the romantic evening has hardly begun.

7. *Harunobu* (1724–1770)

c. 1768. Chuban colour print. c.$9\frac{3}{4} \times 7\frac{1}{2}$in (25 ×19cm)

Harunobu was the first artist to master the potential of the full colour printing technique using multiple, superimposed woodblocks. He has often been praised for the ethereal charm of his slim, fragile beauties. It is not always pointed out that he was also the foremost designer of erotica of his time. In this print he has sketched in just sufficient background to convey the pleasant atmosphere of a summer's afternoon by a country stream. It is worth noting how the printer has managed to show the girl's limbs through the flimsy diaphanous material of her summer dress. The artist's signature appears on the fan.

8. *Koryusai* (active 1766–1788)

c.1770. Chuban colour print. c.9$\frac{3}{4}$ × 7$\frac{1}{2}$in (25 × 19cm)

Koryusai was born a *samurai* in the service of the lord of Tsuchiya and renounced his rank to become a commercial artist. His early work is much influenced by Harunobu, with whom he probably studied. Shortly after Harunobu published his successful *shunga* set, *Maneemon*, in which a diminutive peeper was allowed to glimpse scandalous affairs, Koryusai brought out his own set using a tiny woman as a prying voyeuse. Here she is found sitting on a lacquer *tabako-bon*, beside which a pipe rests abandoned as the lovers lie intertwined, half covered by the folds of a mosquito net.

9. *Koryusai* (active 1766–1788)

c.1775. From 'New patterns for young girls'; oban colour print. c.15 × 9in (38 × 23cm)

Throughout the latter half of the 1770s Koryusai produced a long array of fashion plates showing leading courtesans. There are said to be at least eighty-nine designs from this series alone, and further research may yet reveal more. It was so popular that the publishers later commissioned Kiyonaga and Shunzan to produce further sets with the same title and format. Here the courtesan, Mandayu, is sitting watching her two *kaburo* who are playing *sukeroku*, a dice game in which counters are moved around a board. She is leaning on further games tables, a chequer-board and a *go* table. The containers for the *go* counters are shown on a box on the floor.

10. *Koryusai* (active 1766–1788)

c.1770. Chuban colour print. c.9¾ × 7½in (25 × 19cm)

The sliding wall which separates the wooden-floored corridor, just visible at the bottom left, from the *tatami*, the matted floor covering of the living quarters, has been withdrawn. Concealed from each other's view by a folding screen are two couples. A courtesan and her client are embracing on a striped mattress covered with bed-clothes. His servant, meanwhile, is dallying with her maid, who is plying him with *sake*, which has been warmed in the iron kettle that she is holding.

11. *Koryusai* (active 1766–1788)

c.1770. Chuban colour print. c.9$\frac{3}{4}$ × 7$\frac{1}{2}$in (25 × 19cm)

Koryusai produced a large output of *shunga* characterized by an agile inventiveness of design that never wearies the eye and often surprises by its novel viewpoints. Here we are given an almost bird's-eye view of a couple, entwined, entirely naked, on a mattress on the floor. A maidservant is peeping down at them over the top of a folding screen. The perspective seems extraordinary but serves to make a most effective composition. The almost ubiquitous *tabako-bon* by the bed holds a small container for pieces of live charcoal, with which to light a pipe, and a smaller vessel to take the ashes.

12. *Shunsho* (1726–1792)

1776. From 'A mirror of the fair women of the green houses'; colour-printed book illustration. c.8½ × 12in (21·5 × 30·5cm)

Five courtesans of the Echizen-ya are shown in a relaxed mood amusing themselves by playing *Utagaruta*, a card game in which the object is to match a famous poem with the card showing the portrait of the poet. Each of the girls is named and it would seem that Morokoshi, reclining at the back, has just been caught trying to cheat. This is one illustration from more than forty superb pictures in a three-volume book which was a collaborative work by the artists Shunsho and Shigemasa. Grouped according to the seasons, the designs for summer and winter were contributed by Shunsho, those for spring and autumn by Shigemasa.

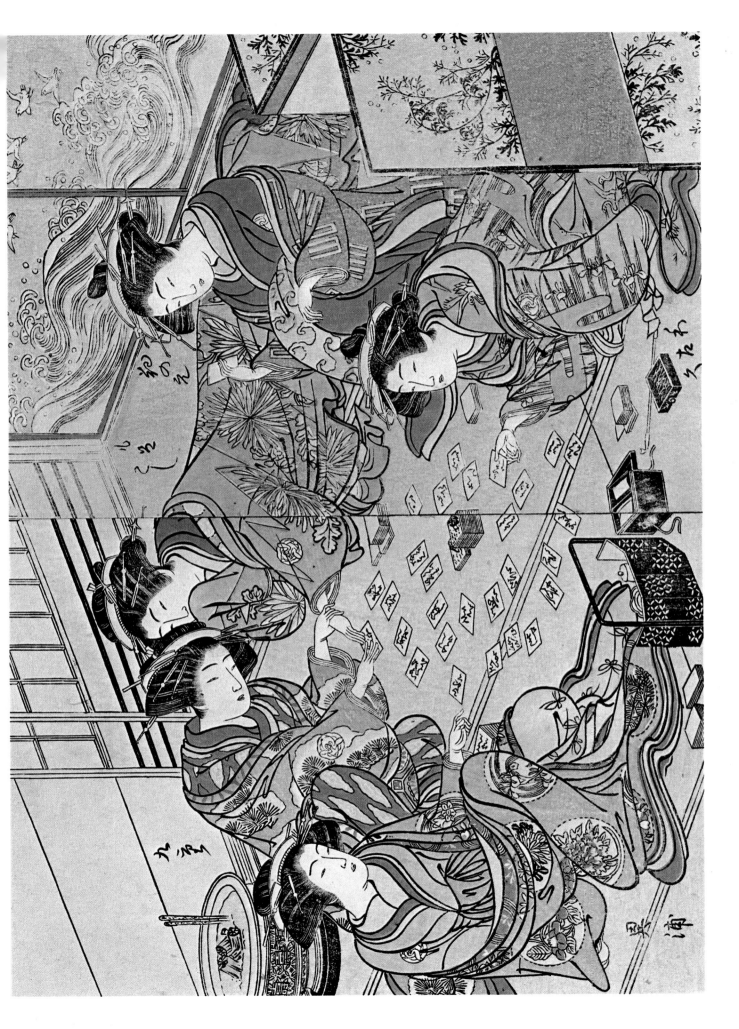

13. *Kiyonaga* (1752–1815)

c.1785. Chuban colour print. c.9¾ × 7½in (25 × 19cm)

The open-air privacy of a balcony offered a favourite
setting for love-making during the hot summer months.
The girl lying in the sun, however, screened from the
awareness of the lovers by the sliding wall, has obviously
decided to remain concealed. It is not uncommon in
shunga to find sexual activity observed by an unperceived
third person. This may be a jealous spouse, an angry
mistress, a lecherous voyeur, a bored servant or,
sometimes, an innocent onlooker unintentionally part of
a scene which politeness dictates should not be
interrupted.

14. *Eishi* (1756–1829)

c.1790. Oban colour prints; two sheets of a triptych.
c.15 × 18in (38 × 46cm)

Inside one of the brothels we find three men, one apparently rather the worse for drink. There are four courtesans with two pink-robed attendants and two *geisha*, Itsuhana and Itsutomi, each with a *samisen*. *Geisha* were entertainers, hired by the hour to provide music and to help the party 'go with a swing', but who were strictly forbidden to trespass on the courtesans' trade. Amid these revellers Eishi has put a host of small allegorical figures. The pleading, anxious little spirits wearing green and white robes have faces composed of the Japanese character, *zen*, or virtue; the taunting, jeering faces of their opponents with pink loin cloths bear the character *aku*, vice. The occupants of the room appear quite oblivious to both.

15. *Kitao Masanobu* (1761–1816)

1784. From 'The autographs of Yoshiwara beauties'; oban colour-printed diptych. c.15 × 18in (38 × 46cm)

An elegant style of calligraphy was much prized in Japan and for the *oiran*, much given to exchanging love-letters with their favourite clients, the possession of an educated and refined script was mandatory. This illustration comes from a superb, large album, in which classical poems, in the handwriting of famous courtesans, are matched with portraits of the girls. The artist was the precocious, witty, fun-loving extrovert Kitao Masanobu. He was only twenty-three when he was commissioned by one of the foremost Edo publishers to design this opulent album. Only a few years later he forsook print design and became famous as an author, a poet and a successful businessman.

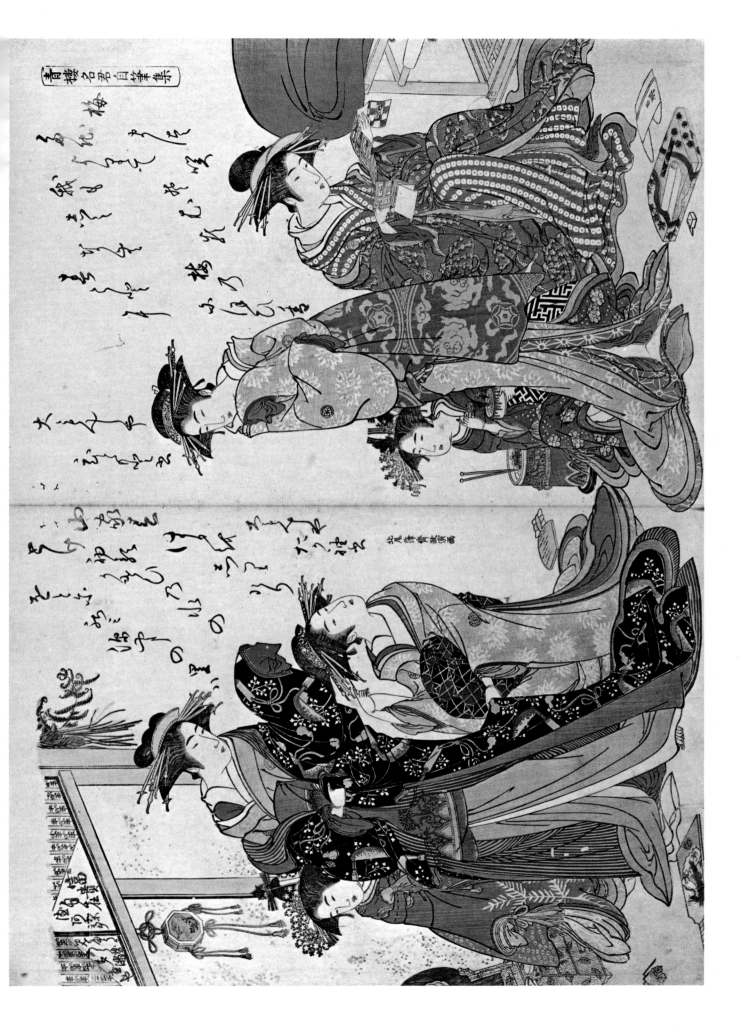

16. *Shuncho* (active 1780–1800)

c.1785. Aiban colour print. c.13$\frac{1}{2}$ × 8$\frac{3}{4}$in (34 × 22cm)

Shuncho, who was Kiyonaga's foremost follower, produced some of the most beautiful erotic pictures of the era. Although it had been Kiyonaga who had established the fashion in *bijin-e* for more naturally robust beauties after the slender, petite girls of Harunobu's generation, it was Shuncho who used the new style to its full advantage in the *shunga* prints and, in this field, he is generally acknowledged to have surpassed his master.

The girl's gesture, raising her sleeve to her mouth, was conventional, implying that she was experiencing emotions that she dare not express vocally. The restrained colouring, known as *beni-girai* (red-avoiding), is typical of some of Shuncho's best work at this time.

17. *Shuncho* (active 1780–1800)

c.1785. Aiban colour print. $13\frac{1}{2} \times 8\frac{3}{4}$in (34 ×22cm)

Shuncho's erotic works frequently place great emphasis on the giving of sexual pleasure. Here the preliminaries are far advanced, the girl is leaning back, eyes closed, her clothes in disarray. The curling of her toes indicates the intensity of her sensations. It is noteworthy that although her state is one of otherwise totally dishevelled abandon, her stylish hair-do, such an important feature of Japanese femininity, remains unaffected. Behind her a folded screen is propped against a bundle of bedding. A tray with bowls of prepared food lies untouched on the floor, and a wad of folded paper tissues is half hidden beneath the folds of her *obi*.

18. *Shuncho* (active 1780–1800)

c.1800. Oban colour print. c.15 × 9in (38 × 23cm)

This impressive bust portrait shows Hanaogi of the Ogi-ya (House of the Fan) which was probably the most famous house in the Yoshiwara (*see also plate 3a*). Certainly Hanaogi (Flower Fan) was the most renowned courtesan of her day. Noted for her beauty, she was also a celebrated poet and calligraphist and was much praised for her special devotion to her elderly mother. She used the house *mon* (emblem), three fans in a circle, which can be seen on her kimono and on one of the combs in her hair.

19. *Shuncho* (active 1780–1800)

c.1785. Aiban colour print. c.13½ ×8¾in (34 ×22cm)

The girl in this print is a courtesan, not from the Yoshiwara, but from the Yagura-shita at Fukagawa, one of the smaller, unlicensed pleasure quarters of Edo. Said to have had a more homely, simple atmosphere than its larger rival, it was favoured by those who liked its relative informality.

The girl's *mon*, a motif of *ginko* blossom, can be seen on the sleeve of her robe and is also shown on the lacquer cabinet behind her and on the padded headrest in the foreground. Such headrests were used, when sleeping, instead of pillows and helped to preserve the hair from disarrangement, the full coiffeur being renewed only about once a week.

20. *Shuncho* (active 1780–1800)

c.1785. From 'The twelve seasons of lovemaking'; oban colour print. c.15 × 9in (38 × 23cm)

One of Shuncho's most distinguished *shunga* sets links the designs to the twelve months. This picture is emblematic of December. On the thirteenth day of the twelfth month there occurred *mainen susuharai*, the annual 'Sweeping Day', a form of spring-cleaning in preparation for the New Year. Clothes have been hung out to air and the girl's brush is lying on the floor, disregarded where it fell when she was interrupted.

21. *Toyokuni* (1769–1825)

*1802. From 'Modern figures of fashion'; colour-printed
book illustration. c.7½ × 10½in (19 × 26·5cm)*

We are taken behind the scenes at the Yoshiwara to see
a group of five girls of the third grade relaxing in their
living quarters. The mirror in a lacquer box on a stand,
the *samisen* hanging from a hook on the wall and the
bundles of clothing and bedding draped over a rail or
strewn on the floor, serve to strike a note of domesticity.
By the window two girls are discussing a long love
letter, with paper and a tray of writing materials beside
them on the floor. In the centre a girl is proudly
displaying her arm, tattooed with the name of her
current lover.

22. *Utamaro* (1754–1806)

c.1800. Oban colour print. 15 × 9in (38 × 23cm)

While the dutiful Japanese wife might sometimes envy the *oiran* her fashionable life in the pleasure quarters, the courtesan must frequently have yearned for the stable tranquillity of married life. Utamaro has shown us a girl, her face half covered by a transparent green fan, dozing over a book and dreaming of her wedding procession. The inset draws an analogy with the legend of Rosei, a Chinese scholar who fell asleep on a magic pillow and dreamed of honours heaped on him by a grateful Emperor, only to wake disillusioned.

23. *Utamaro* (1754–1806)

c.1793. Oban colour print. c.15 × 9in (38 × 23cm)

During the early 1790s competition between publishers of prints of beautiful girls seems to have reached fever pitch. A succession of eye-catching techniques were evolved and here, a glowing, plain yellow ground helps offset the simplicity of this courtesan at her toilet. Her hair, freshly washed, has been casually pinned up prior to its styling. A white cosmetic has already been applied to the face and neck and her teeth have been blackened. With a slight frown of concentration she is applying lip-rouge with a brush, carefully studying the result in a hand mirror.

24. *Utamaro* (1754–1806)

c.1793. From 'Pictures of beauties making up'; oban colour print. c.15 × 9in (38 × 23cm)

Japanese male cynics said that the looking glass was the mind of a woman. As a theme, the pretty girl and her mirror was repeated by artist after artist. None succeeded better than Utamaro's brilliant design shown here. The use of burnished mica to highlight the glass of the mirror was one of his most impressive effects, using a technique which was then the height of fashion with the print-buying public. The result is certainly one of his finest prints.

We know that this print must have been popular, since at least two editions are recorded. The other version, otherwise identical, has the series title *A mirror of seven persons hairdressing* and shows a *mon* of paulownia blossom on the girl's sleeve.

25. *Utamaro* (1754–1806)

c.1793. From 'Six crystal rivers'; oban colour print.
c.15 × 9in (38 × 23cm)

The courtesan Hana-murasaki (Violet Flower) of the
Kado-tama-ya is sitting gazing at the mirror held for her
by her attendant. The six 'Crystal Rivers' of the title were
renowned for their limpid clarity and each was
traditionally linked to a poem from the classical
anthologies. In this instance the poem, by Toshiyori
(twelfth century), starts 'Tomorrow we shall come again
to the crystal river by the meadow-path, where the
bush-clover grows . . .' and the allusion is portrayed in
the pattern on the girl's robe. Further, in the circular
cartouche above, an apt contemporary poem reads, 'Ah
me, the lover that promises to come again tomorrow!
He is like a wave gliding on Tama stream' (trans.
Laurence Binyon), which gives a rather sad flavour to
this beautiful print.

26. *Utamaro* (1754–1806)

c.1795. From 'The twelve hours of the green houses'; oban colour print. c.15 × 9in (38 × 23cm)

The twelve hours of the green houses, one of Utamaro's most impressive sets, shows courtesans and their daily round of activities. In Japan the hours of daylight and darkness were each divided into six periods of about two hours, each designated by a sign of the zodiac. This is the hour of the Monkey (3pm–5pm) and the famous courtesan Hanaogi (see also *plate 18*) is shown on her afternoon parade through the Yoshiwara with her *shinzo* and *kaburo*. The latter is almost completely hidden, only the top of her head and her hair decorations being just visible above Hanaogi's *obi*. The title cartouche is in the form of a bracket-clock with a bell above and two counterweights suspended on cords beneath.

27. *Utamaro* (1754–1806)

c.1795. From 'The twelve hours of the green houses'; oban colour print. c.15 × 9in (38 × 23cm)

From the same series as *plate 26*, this represents the hour of the Cock (5pm–7pm). A courtesan, summoned to an assignation, is preparing to set out accompanied by a servant with a lantern. The lantern, which folds down like a concertina to allow the wick to be lit, is being pulled up towards the retaining hook. It bears the device of the three fans in a circle, the *mon* of the Ogi-ya (House of the Fan).

The elegance of the tall, slender courtesan, accentuated by the contrast with the maidservant, is typical of this splendid set. The designs are superbly printed and stand out against a yellow background sprinkled with gold dust.

28. *Utamaro* (1754–1806)

1788. From 'The poem of the pillow'; oban colour print.
c.15 ×9in (38 ×23cm)

One of Utamaro's best-known, earliest, most beautiful
erotic albums carried part of his name punningly in its
title, *Uta-makura*, 'The Poem of the Pillow'. The pictures
are full of emotional intensity and dramatic contrasts.
The designs are brilliantly conceived and the colours and
printing are technically superb.

   A couple are making love on a balcony. He is watching
her intently as she tenderly caresses his cheek. His hand
is resting on the nape of her neck, an area of special
erotic interest for the Japanese. His fan, held casually
open, is inscribed with a poem which compares his
position to a bird, its beak trapped in a bivalve shell,
unable to fly away.

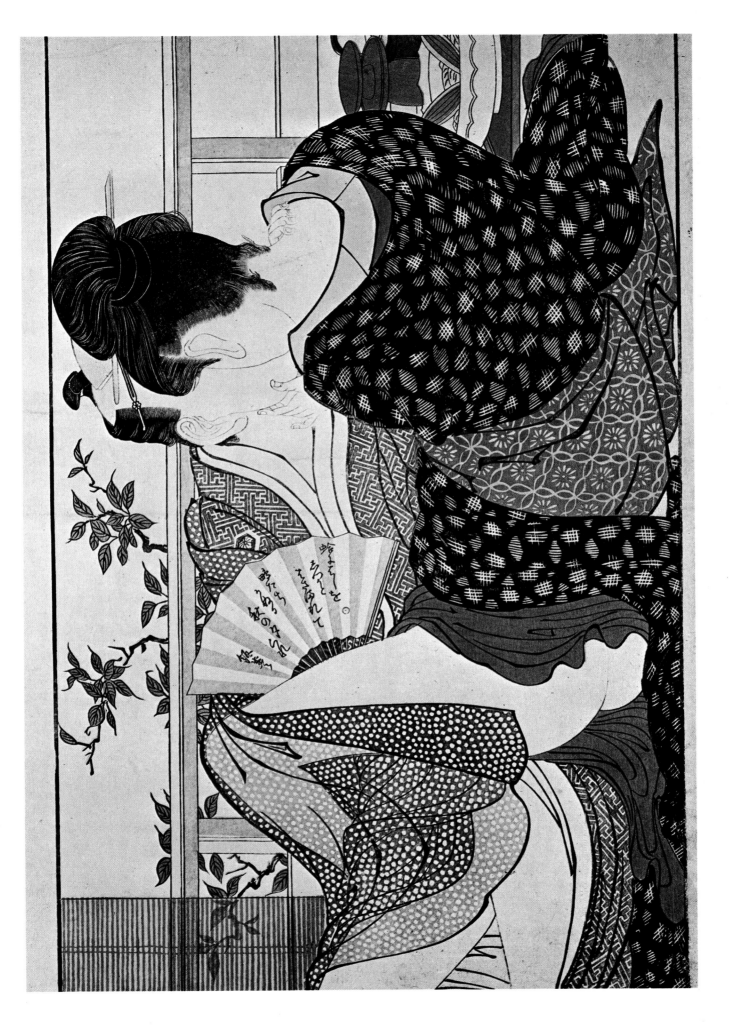

29. *Utamaro* (1754–1806)

1788. From 'The poem of the pillow'; oban colour print.
c.15 × 9in (38 × 23cm)

The *Utamakura* is characterized by the way that it
portrays the range of emotions potentially involved when
love and passion are aroused. Here anger and jealousy
on the part of the woman, sparked off by finding a love-
letter from an unsuspected rival, have interrupted their
rendezvous. The way that she clutches at his kimono
and the tell-tale dishevelment of her hair bespeak the
intensity of her emotions, unappeased by his defensive
gesture of placation. Behind her a black iron kettle
stands on a tripod on a charcoal brazier.

30. *Utamaro* (1754–1806)

*1788. From 'The poem of the pillow'; oban colour print.
c.15 × 9in (38 × 23cm)*

This beautifully balanced composition shows Utamaro at
his best. In the background, standing screens decorated
with plum blossom and bamboo provide straight lines
and acute angles to contrast with the flowing curves of
the lovers. By cutting off part of the design at the bottom
and allowing part of the man's top-knot to protrude out
of the picture at the top the artist gives us the impression
of close physical involvement in the scene.

31. *Utamaro* (1754–1806)

*1788. From 'The poem of the pillow'; oban colour print.
c.15 × 9in (38 × 23cm)*

The crisp clarity of the superb printing, characteristic of
this album, helps to convey the open air freshness in this
picture of lovers under a tree in springtime. In the
distance small green hillocks are surmounted by
flowering cherry trees. As usual, special attention is paid
to the girl's fashionable patterned clothing. The design of
chrysanthemum blooms on the *obi* is particularly
effective. She is holding a wad of paper tissues in her
left hand.

32. *Eisho* (active 1789–1801)

c.1795. From 'A comparison of beauties within the enclosure'; oban colour print. c.15 ×9in (38 ×23cm)

Eisho is the most commonly encountered artist of the small but talented group under the tutelage of Eishi, and this striking, half-length portrait is typical of his best work. The courtesan Kasugano of the Sasa-ya is shown using a fold of her loose bath-wrap to dry her neck. The bold, stellate, printed pattern of the cotton was obviously very fashionable at the time as several other artists, including Utamaro, illustrated similarly patterned materials at about the same date.

33. *Eisho* (active 1789–1801)

c.1800. From 'Models of calligraphy'; oban colour print.
c.15 × 9in (38 × 23cm)

In spite of a policy of excluding all foreigners from their islands, the Japanese allowed a small Dutch colony at Nagasaki. This proved a useful trading post for the Japanese government and a source of continual wonder and curiosity for the ordinary Japanese people. It is not common to find foreigners depicted in *shunga* and, in this case, the design is clearly based on that of a Dutch couple by Utamaro in the *Uta-makura* of a dozen years before. Emphasis is placed on the outlandish garb, the long fingernails and the luxuriant beard and moustaches of this 'hairy barbarian'. A wisp of fragrant smoke rises from an incense burner on the small European table.

34. *Kuniyasu* (1794–1832)

c.1830. Oban colour print. c.15 × 9in (38 × 23cm)

The three-stringed *samisen* was the most popular musical
instrument for everyday entertainment. It was played
using a plectrum such as that in this girl's right hand.
In her other hand she is carrying a wad of paper tissues
and one of the shallow cups used for serving *sake*, the
rice wine which was usually drunk hot and which was
a feature of any festive gathering. She is wearing a
kimono patterned with *chidori*, a species of plover which
the Japanese said was born from the froth off the crests
of waves.

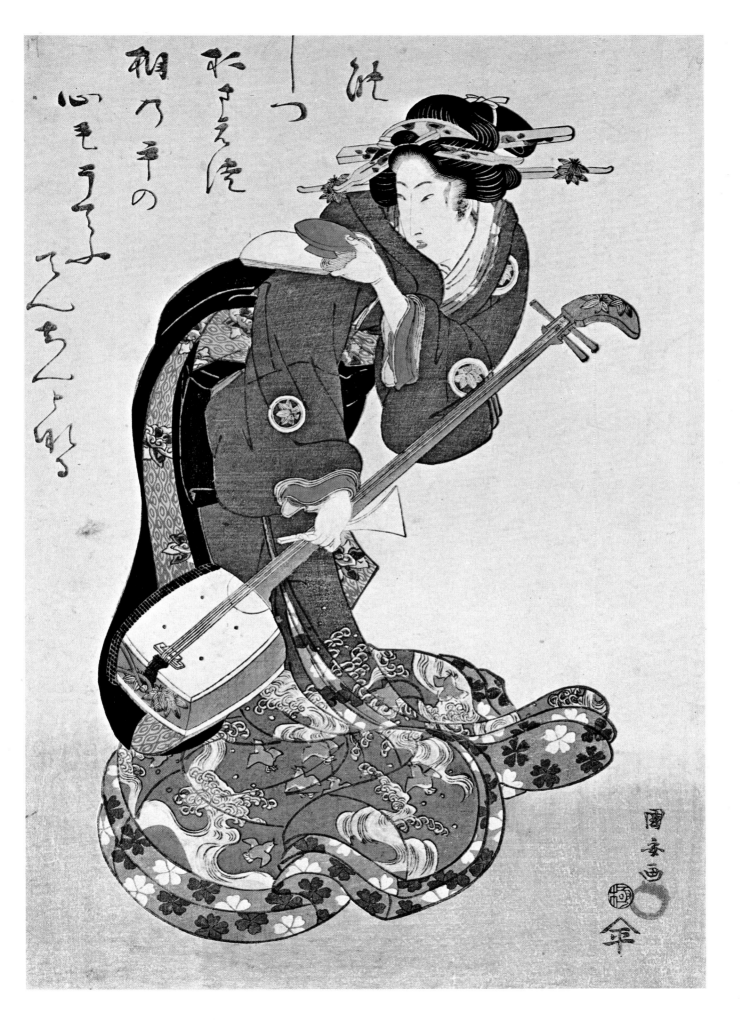

35. *Kikumaru* (active 1795–1818)

c.1800. Oban colour print. c.15 × 9in (38 × 23cm)

The formal ritual of preparing and serving the specially ground green tea used in the tea-ceremony required a strict adherence to etiquette. Originally part of a refined aesthetic cult linked with Zen ideals in which a small party of nobles and literati would meet in seclusion, it later became popular in an attenuated form for those with pretensions to cultural pursuits. Here the courtesan Ainare, an inmate of the Kado-ebi-ya, is polishing a tea bowl. Before her lie some of the implements needed for the ceremony: a bamboo ladle on a special stand; a thin sliver of bamboo used for spooning the powdered tea balancing on a crystal bowl; a split bamboo whisk with which to mix the tea into a froth; and a crackle-glaze porcelain water-jar.

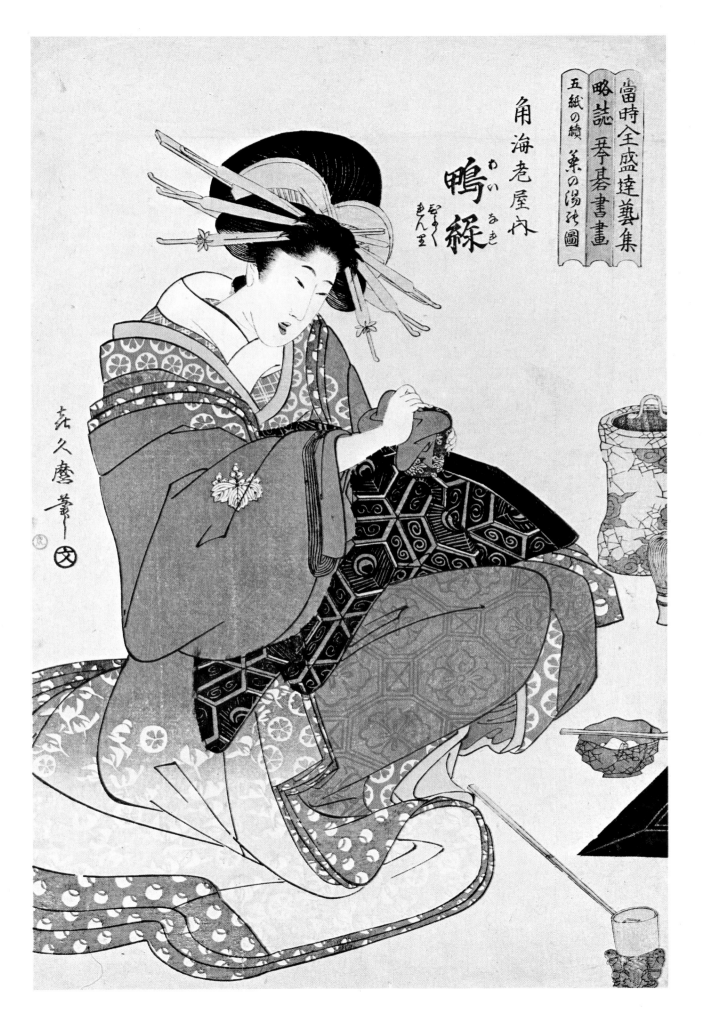

36. *Eizan* (1787–1867)

*c.1815. From 'Tamanoto meisho monogatari'; colour-
printed book illustration. c.6 × 8in (15 × 20·5cm)*

This erotic guide book places sexual encounters in noted
beauty spots. In this scene the artist has placed the lovers
in the garden of a famous river-side tea-house. The
whole scene is bathed in moonlight. The verandah is lit
by paper lanterns and through the translucent paper of
the walls can be seen the silhouettes of the revellers
within, singing, drinking and dancing to the music of
the *samisen*. Such a scene would have been very
evocative to the pleasure-loving citizens of Edo.

37. *Kuniyoshi* (1798–1861)

1837. From 'Flowers with abundant benefits'; colour-printed book illustration. $7 \times 5\frac{1}{4}$in (18 × 13·5cm)

This frontispiece to a *shunga* book shows a girl at her toilet. In contrast to the pictures of courtesans with their splendid robes, Kuniyoshi shows us the figure of a bare-backed girl. The print is skilfully designed to concentrate attention on her neck, and must have had particular impact and appeal at the time. The nape of the neck, one of the few parts of a Japanese woman which was usually uncovered, had a special erotic interest and fascination for the Japanese. The fine draughtsmanship and superb composition are typical of this artist, who was one of the great print designers of the nineteenth century.

38. *Kuniyoshi* (1798–1861)

*c.1855. From Komoncho, 'A notebook of small patterns';
colour-printed book illustration. c.7½ × 10½in (19 × 26·5cm)*

All passion is spent. The scattered bedclothes and the
used tissues tell their tale. The satiated girl lies with a
languorous half-smile, her eyes closed, while her lover
leans under the mosquito curtain to pour out a cup of
tea. Seldom has the aftermath of relaxed and happy
love-making been more strikingly portrayed. Kuniyoshi
was one of the most prolific and popular artists of the
second quarter of the nineteenth century. He illustrated
more than forty *shunga* books. One of the finest of these,
Komoncho was published in three volumes, each
containing about half a dozen of his best erotic designs.

39. *Utamaro* (1754–1806)

1804. From 'Annals of the green houses'; colour-printed book illustration. c.$7\frac{1}{2} \times 10\frac{1}{2}$in (19 $\times$26·5cm)

This print shows daybreak in the Yoshiwara and the revelry and passion is over. Amid the early morning bustle screens are being rearranged, the brazier is stirred into fresh life and tea is being prepared. Isolated and aloof now, the customer is sitting on a ledge by the window, staring out at the snow softly falling in the grey dawn outside.

40. *Hokusai* (1760–1849)

1821. From 'Manpoku wago-jin'; colour-printed book illustration. $7\frac{1}{2} \times 5\frac{1}{4}$ in (19 × 13·25cm)

The wide-ranging talent and eccentric, intensely individual style of Hokusai dominated the art of the Japanese print throughout the first third of the nineteenth century. In this picture, the frontispiece to one of his best erotic books, he personified the sex organs as a paunchy couple, standing on a rocky shore, affectionately holding hands, their arms around each other's shoulders.

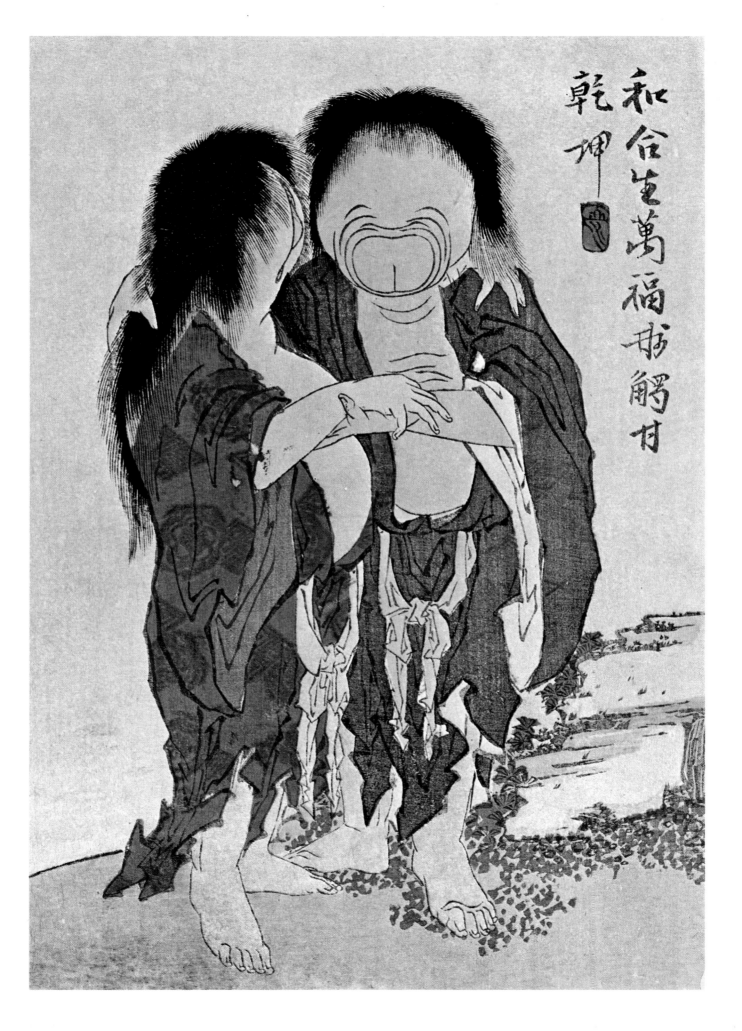

Acknowledgements

THE AUTHOR AND BLACKER CALMANN COOPER LTD would like to thank the museums and collectors who allowed works in their collections to be reproduced in this book, including the British Museum (plates 2, 22, 23, 25, 26, 27, 28) and the Victoria and Albert Museum (plates 9, 15, 18, 32, 34, 35).